OUTREMER

Outremer

POEMS BY BILL KNOTT

UNIVERSITY OF IOWA PRESS

IOWA CITY

University of Iowa Press, Iowa City 52242
Printed in the United States of America
First edition, 1989

Design by Richard Hendel
Typesetting by G&S Typesetters,
Austin, Texas
Printing and binding by Thomson-Shore,
Dexter, Michigan

Earlier versions of some of these poems
appeared in the following magazines:
Quarry West, Seneca Review, Caliban, and
Exquisite Corpse.

Library of Congress
Cataloging-in-Publication Data

Knott, Bill, 1940–
    Outremer: poems/Bill Knott.—1st ed.
      p.   cm.—(Iowa poetry prize)
    ISBN 0-87745-254-7,
    ISBN 0-87745-255-5 (pbk.)
    I. Title. II. Series.
PS3561.N6509   1989   89-33146
811'.54—dc20   CIP

DEDICATION

to James Tate

Publication of this book

was made possible by a

generous grant from

the University of Iowa

Foundation

CONTENTS

PART ONE

Endless Evening: My Life at Il Vittoriale / 1
Fernand Khnopff / 2
John Gray / 3
Pornokrates / 4
February Fourteenth: Freezeframe / 5
Barren Precinct / 6
Vague Consoles / 7
Alfonsina Storni / 8
Art or the Caresses or the Sphinx (Castration Envy #36) / 9
Sadak in Search of the Waters of Oblivion / 10
Eros and Espionage in the Bent Center / 11
Castration Envy #12 (Collected Portraits of the Marchesa Casati) / 12
Costarring Oscar Wilde as Madame Sosostris / 13
(Let Me Take You on a) Sea Breeze / 14
Nun Claims Most Snakes Too Serious to Make Good Bookmarks
    (Your Soul Is a Chosen Landscape) / 15
My Plea for Sanctum in the Sculpture Garden of Medusa / 16

PART TWO

An Afternoon with Eugenio / 19
Our Catacomb's Next Martyr / 20
Suicidal Thoughts on Being Refused a Guggenheim Grant
    for the 11th Time / 21
The Golden Age / 22
The Words to the Title / 23
Weltende Variation #1 / 24
Childhood: The Offense of History / 25

After Breton Expels Me from the Group, I Go down on Samson
    and Delilah / 26
The Code / 27
Last Stop before Poem / 28
(Castration Envy #21) Does the Swordswallower Shit
    Plowshares? / 29
Euclid Alone / 30
Night and the Naked / 31
I Meet an Andy / 32
Help / 33
My Epitaph / 33
Poem! / 33
Psychopathology of the Powertool Weekend (Neocolonialism #5) / 34
Mother Teresa Treats Terrorists to Taffy / 35
De President of Descent (Neocolonialism #16) / 36

PART THREE

Male Menopause Poem / 39
Castration Envy #11 / 40
School for Insomnia / 41
A Virginsaint and a Saintvirgin Share a Halo a While: A Memory / 42
Up to the Minute / 43
Alphabetical Morning / 44
For Imelda Marcos / 45
Last Moments in the Masterpiece / 46
More Best Jokes of the Delphic Oracle / 47
Hitler Skeleton Goldplated (From *Treasures of the C.I.A. Museum*,
    edited by Hilton Kramer, with an Introduction by Jerzy Kosinski.
    Random House/IBM, 1984) / 48
Auto-renga / 49
No Androgyne Is an Archipelago / 50
Nonrequitals / 51
The Heroes Crowd Each Other at the Gate / 52

The Frootloops of Consolation / 53
At the Nixon Memorial / 54
The Sculpture / 55
Brighton Rock by Graham Greene / 56
Refusing an Invitation to the Masked Ball / 58

Notes on Poems / 59

Pilgrims who came to the Holy Land were often shocked by the luxury and license of life in Outremer.

—M. R. B. Shaw,
Chronicles of the Crusades

PART ONE

Let us go hence—the night is now at hand . . .

—Dowson

ENDLESS EVENING:
MY LIFE AT IL VITTORIALE

For caught in those Aug-Sept hours what day can
Break this slang of glass whose illustration
Of flotsam sampling our poison's portion of calm
Lives long the lament we swore applause by.

With faster than flashbacks in a promo for
Memory to lie lymph along these hits of hope
And through each thought we just dawned on interrupt
Poses no soprano care counterfeit or water yet.

As though it alone the profile were wielded up
To shield the face against that bad vocable our own
Throws veils another pale divulge of oh mise en moon.

Musingly to see a bed on fire in a huge room
Otherwise empty while one at a time
White sheets float down from somewhere onto the flames.

FERNAND KHNOPFF

Days in the lull, gathered afternoon of it,
—A touch of star-decals on one's bookbag,—
Silence, like a vast confetti of souls, and that
Torporic breeze: oh how difficult

The culling of love from our facades is.
Once, never to go the cling thing seemed what's
Sublimest. Look at those cobwebcrobats,
Skittering skyward, fingerhold, nor toe- .

Deep down (in my ugh-roots) I longed to brag
My spiel shall deign define no July of these.
I'll fall chapter closed across your chest is all.

Now I am an atrocious expert; who answers
Every question by, "It is very simple:
We must listen to Beauty with frozen ears."

I try to tonguejob a languagejob you
You continue to perfect the anonymity
Of your first and final lovers or is that me
I try to occupy my debris till I see.

Are we the cow that swallowed the hymen Jesus
Spat out at birth for example-psych or
Dorian's portrait faced off with a virgin mirror
Is that what Life Beyond The Baton is like.

A disservice to myself is my head
The kind of divingboard that slices bread
They gnawed the renowned for fun they said.

Where the linger of one thought longer than
An other brings distress will this settle gelid
Its aspic of aspect make ick my eye.

PORNOKRATES
(homage Felicien Rops)

We paged through the phrase as though it were ours.
—The lovers in the act—those de Sade-laden hours,
Who, dumped out daily as ashtrays this dream
Some room's motel, will it burn a hole here too—

And coop us full of that till our limbs' arms
Chainsmoked by adrenalin, slither dour-white
Unepitaphed beds but. What gargoyle jail
Their contortion poses (the lovers in the act

Of mailing themselves to famous crimes) if
(Where perched on each other's tongues we fly)
Only by his mind these bodies thrash—

To share this fire is, surely, a tithe entire.
So each of us alone unless upon our lips
The world forgets our name and stammers out its.

FEBRUARY FOURTEENTH: FREEZEFRAME

(to James Elroy Flecker, with thanks for translating teardrops into handcuffs)

Please press a valentine shape tool to my chest
And extract from it what was never there
Then singe your ciggie on this thing that mists
Over only when shattered 's no mirror

I lie beside you my caresses deepmeant
Though they fade as fast as escape plans traced
Across a prison blanket by an absent
Fingernail whose blood you piss in my face

Is that it is that why I cry for your torture
That way you look at me pityingly
Iffen I say things like rain ice drops cling

There our branch out there like someone been trying
On all their bracelets at once to see
Which is prettiest but of course none are

BARREN PRECINCT
(homage Hagiwara Sakutarō)

Tightropes cross swayingly from church belfry
to church belfry, in one street a pileup of mattresses
is burning. If it were snowing it would be
like their very first sheets returning,
fresh from the sky's laundry. In the bracingly cold air
I see doorframes with no houses, houses with no rooms, and houses
where they serve lunch in its most naive form. I amble toward
a wood fence, a childishly-chalked bullseye, in which
I find some kind of old military medal pinned dead center:
the medal has a pale, harmful ribbon; it flutters and or
     rattles whitely, whitely withstanding the wind,
defending the bullseye's secret, inmost ring.
If cornered, I would agree—with almost no argument—:
this medal should get a medal!

Barren precinct,
eyes stare at you without our even knowing,
like the statue of a buddha
they regard you with immobilized eyes, with
carven idol eyelids,
you are the eternal non-unguent of tearless eyes,
the blink that will never be.

VAGUE CONSOLES

This vista often awarded John Ford his rest.
Myself, scenery has a lack of I (emphasis).
And haven't we killed all the Indians yet?
In a stagecoach—made of sagebrush, no doubt—,

I would gauche-out like a tumbleweed at a sockhop.
Yo, watch it roll across the old gym-floor, loboto
Basketball: then, toed by foetid teens, fall,
Slo-mo, as though some flair for the vague consoles—

Oh lips, refusing their tongues' rights, bodies
Trying to put down the peaceful demands of
Their genitalia . . . yes everything looks better shot

Through John Wayne's hurt. The sky the way it mattes—
The desert. A lone rider, whose moral I await.
The crotches arranging themselves for death.

Feeling as you wrote that the cancer quote
Is on its way upstairs   to the throat
One breast had already flown   migrant
Heart   de facto amazon   only the sea remained

Like a jealous mattress an   old pillow stuffed
With insomnia's phonebills the sea
Is there to throw oneself at   at dawn   late
Up all night over   a poem called Voy a

Dormir and which says   this   better than this
(Each time I read one by you I revise
Myself my suicide is   to be me instead of you)

Sea that swallowed your poet   throat
Does not   for the having of it   sing less
And besides   only that cancer tried to float

ART OR THE CARESSES
OR THE SPHINX
(CASTRATION ENVY #36)

The Lord Peter Mumsey of Thebes, that yummy
Oedi-poo dick, advises me, It's no use. To
Detectify a guilty party will
Soil the purity of our respective plagues.

Like a silo filled with silhouettes of sigh
I reply. My smarm, your frissonpassion
To be eliminated from the world's
Verticalities are more of what photons do

To phaetons. Therefore, if that obliteracy
Our face slash esperanto saliva
Trace or clue is left to sift through but this

Issuey stuff, whoa, who's to blame, us! So I whore
Is for sure and if death occurs, facile
Excel. 'What's named between the knees' 's not me.

SADAK IN SEARCH OF
THE WATERS OF OBLIVION

Is my Way to be crushed between your old
Testament and your new while the flood-blond
Of my major attributes burns, insurgent
And scrupulous beast? That epileptics'

Trigger phrase your name rages each page or
Are those foams yanked from among my teeth
Mere suicides giggling in a mudbath perhaps—
Only the beach leaps at lapses of itself.

To swab my pittance with this is heartless.
—And yet these traces of an unfaithful navel
In the sand sign Go mode as, vast pilgrim,

You undo my i.d. so skillfully:—
Rollcall of absence whose program runs
Through all veins! Oh sea. Besieged by ilk, I am.

EROS AND ESPIONAGE IN
THE BENT CENTER
*(for Helen C----n, after reading
D. G. Rossetti's "Troy Town")*

More undermined by your meander than my thirst
From wine's first cup what shard still tastes this milk
Above whom shone a normal polaroid of the void
A song saliva cannot tie its envious vines to

Shall I paint through all the Isms to show you
Bricabrac from that breast fill worlds marked sale-price
Yet conceptualists slumming in the real congeal
Is here a thing to say of this say or said place

Now the merry-go-round it goes-a-round old 'Troy Town'
My bed hangs out the window by its toes shouting
Each day your hair strays across such ruins

But to live live simply in compress with our time
TV-star footprints to immortalize sidewalk
Me slurp your sweetpuddle up out of an autograph

CASTRATION ENVY #12
(COLLECTED PORTRAITS OF
THE MARCHESA CASATI)

The knifefighter's mouth on my cancelled flesh
While, mutinous, tincan-incommunicado, I
—Or in that psycho syringe my face, all
The thawed camel of my eyes, the ball

Point pen pickling in my anus writes poem:
Trapped by titular star-wince, is it sky
I always escape from, to make the lam my home . . . hmm?
Unless my blood—like some more intimate

Form of ivy cover it—blond abattoir
Where a loincloth contemplates emptiness
Or less. Slash-wounds they should rename me for.

My gordian sex axed solves one puzzle though
I hesitate still, to give this portrait
A sign. Pool of saliva under the mistletoe?

COSTARRING OSCAR WILDE
AS MADAME SOSOSTRIS

White, white as a tablecloth that moonlights as a bride
For the unborn you—appeared—or a waterfall
Which leaned against another waterfall (your hair).
My beeper slave of lost voices barked: what?

Whole the cup that knelt to summer burst; I tried
To garden the fireplace and farm the doormat
But proto-frog-photos of you grew to lieu me there
Groping with bare hands of flood my gnarlgargoyle.

Deeper than my beeper you knew; sibyled guesses.
And yet . . . 'misery is proximity'. Oh
The seance was as far as possible tuxedoes.

Aftermath is a mouth. Speaks. Speaks? Yes, but less as
Flesh than what; yak mask for that old fop Apollo?
The god retrieves his gloves
                              and, feigning to go, goes.

(LET ME TAKE YOU ON A)
SEA BREEZE

Our flesh so tender so turnstile
Plus on top of that everything addressed
To that Occupant within me are read
Gauguin/Kerouac comes to mind.

Empty passim one more Day One passes
The field abandoned to handstands
Superfluous lay all waters in that gaze
Guiles of a map guess-gestured.

I'll become a crematory prostitute
The prom whose bra undressed my ears
None us dispedestal that idol.

Or what better yet a desert island
Sailed to only by blind sailors who smile
Like swans we maim our bracelets in.

NUN CLAIMS MOST SNAKES
TOO SERIOUS TO MAKE GOOD
BOOKMARKS (YOUR SOUL
IS A CHOSEN LANDSCAPE)

A la gongs, that await the Emperor's semen
But in vain, I partition silence into rooms
Called poems. Why? Only Empresses remain—
Is this too apropos: should seed, blown from some

Sunflower come to land solely on sun dials . . .
Yet wig of compass-needles; comet. Soars
—For sync's sake? Like optional hearts, in styles
Singular averse against the opus wall of stars

Spring safetypins my penis to my navel,
Praying that so fetal a petal shall shrivel still:
A thank-silence follows; a field day feeling;

Queen Staypower paints out our scene's see-me's
(Dream-prussic pupils flare—flush with their irises).
The sun wonderlands it all a bit, by falling.

MY PLEA FOR SANCTUM IN THE
SCULPTURE GARDEN OF MEDUSA

A statue's first pedestal is the stone
It was cut from out in. Those are just words though.
Like: Spring! then death puts on the wrong clothes . . .
Then air ruts flushed as bathtub sex, as . . . proseate?

Because, that prince of an ostrich Narcissus
His embedded-headed gaze upon his
Twin the corpse Hamlet proposed, posing for those
Snapshoticisms is so, so 'real-ergo-vile', less

Tangent than tangible, hell.
                              —*Till I stand*
In Her garden's one among many I can only
Torment vesanic vanities/age-of-oh orbs where

Deep in the honor of my ether I soar, where
—Passing at high mimicries through the night
I go, all lop-worlded and alone, to kill abandon.

PART TWO

I know not in what metal I have wrought;
Nor whether what I fashion will be thrust
Beneath the clods that hid forgotten thought;

But if it is of gold it will not rust . . .

—*Lee-Hamilton*

But how boring. And so, the rain was of use . . .
that window ratatat threw my smiles' drift.
Thimbledown heavy its downplay lasted for hours;
were the core seasons flowering, no longer
believing that to die that way, sated
in that cloud-loud debate, in that nacre-null sky,
would (finally) reify more gender: stars, all
those birthday elements, the bare *paysage*
of a blaze too logical for our headlines, massed,
or shed the odd ganglia we misname them by . . .
And this despite those arriviste freighters—
and in the harbor, no less! Gilded grew
each porthole's penny of envy. But now
Damocles' last wig smacks down, toward the mouth
of Etna whose wisest cigarette-lighter (lifted
from the giftshoppe there) strikes flameless
three times in a row: trick omen, infernal feign, and so.
Unless the rain can be blamed, this ratatat rain:
gun that aims my fingers at my thumb—instead of him.

The demonic city, the wretchedness of suburbs,
Bodies fished out of rivers, and distress
In the hospitals are also on my list.
(Oh blindfold-anointed night, Nero Nixon nevermore.)

Waiting for dawn to X-rate the sky. Love. Love—
The trendsetters yawn over their trendsets—
Hey, Hiroshima: duck! While the fuck of it
Sucks a crucifix stuck in the rat-hole door

Of the secret vault where a Getty gloats
Whole floors of masterpieces, real Mona Lisa and all.
In curtseyland I'll take my stand he screams.

The sound blood makes dripping on their neon
Must of bored the crowd. Facade-trod face of:
Inflect with your name time sours my knees.

SUICIDAL THOUGHTS ON
BEING REFUSED A GUGGENHEIM
GRANT FOR THE 11TH TIME

War headlines/peace tailstanzas don't
Like to feel real. Scare tactics take practice
So that, institutionally, a wine corked
By the horn of a charging unicorn might?

The fur opens and my face ain't.
The fur closes: eyes lips nose resume
The wretched perfection of feature-ifice
The dumbpan plan, identity, lack of choice.—

I cling to virgin, this veil scrape(d) surface
Where our scars are an armor of absence
What knight attains: ignore

That pig-bladder matter, life, that failure
Dangled in whiskey like a longshot tooth.
The night has no thoughts heavier than itself.

is thought to be a confession, won by endless
torture, but which our interrogators must
hate to record—all those old code names, dates,
the standard narrative of sandpaper
throats, even its remorse, fall ignored. Far

away, a late (not lost) messenger stares,
struck by window bargains or is it the gift
of a sudden solicitude: is she going to
lift up her shadow's weight, shift hers
onto it? She knows who bears whom. In

that momentary museum where memory occurs
more accrue of those torturers' pincers than
lessened fingernails, eyes teased to a pulp,
we beg for closeups. *Ormolus, objets d'art!*
A satyr drains an hourglass with one gulp.

From my eye is plot a tear that contains
The odd-numbered waves
Of a lost ocean
That writes help on a thought then throws it

Through the window of a floating handmirror
Some mimes
Passed among themselves while drowning
Sharing it back and forth like a fun book

From my eye is paint a tear that stains
Those splash-grasped pages
Unbled-black inks
White-subtle faces

Enjambed beneath these even waves that lay
Solitaire on the sand
Where I stand crying
Trying to remember the words to the title

WELTENDE VARIATION #1
(homage Jacob van Hoddis)

The CIA and the KGB exchange Christmas cards
A blade snaps in two during an autopsy
The bouquet Bluebeard gave his first date reblooms
Many protest the public stoning of a guitar pick

Railroad trains drop off the bourgeois' pointy head
A martyr sticks a coffeecup out under a firehose
Moviestars make hyenas lick their spaceship
God's hand descends into a glove held steady by the police

At their reunion The New Faces recognize each other
A spoiled child sleeps inside a thermometer
A single misprint in a survival manual kills everyone
The peace night makes according to the world comes

CHILDHOOD: THE OFFENSE OF HISTORY

Scraping a poised enough patina of voyeur
From your eye I spread peanut butter on my
Groin and let the ocean waves wash it off—
Hey, nice cosmic microdots. For afters we'll

Listlessly memorize the Smith wing in
The phone book or try to hump Empty Dumpty: vain
Efforts that crud up what we have done
In obscure countries driven by passion

Out onto balconies to address the
Populace with our love, false solution
For their poverty which is based on

The art that the dirt in my heart is white.
Crammed mad, thoughtmotes in a themebeam:
He has a shiv grin. The soap he uses is ugly.

AFTER BRETON EXPELS ME FROM THE GROUP, I GO DOWN ON SAMSON AND DELILAH

The moon long undue to none of us follows
Typifying some life we phonetically loathe
Or other dolls umbilical to our desires
Let my lips fizz out against your thighs.

The annuities of these nymphs are so paid
But can our praiseworth's cry concur
Pilgrimage-many the tidepools oppose
Sigh only my hemline has aspirations.

Typecast as fat Tantalus/as the last
Frame of an hourglass movie I yawn for more
Bouffant-slut roles roles with grunge-rapport.

Therefore a rumor-millioned perfumes inject
Each of my pores must emit its own odor
If we are to synchronize all earth's sundials.

THE CODE
(for Heather McHugh)

All while I tried to brain myself
With my key-ring
Which unfortunately
Was one shy of being fatal

The fickle key itself lay
In infamy
In the hands of my wife
Who as I fell the blood

Making my forehead
Squeak against the floor
Slid open the secret drawer

Of my escritoire
That's weird she said
He uses real names in his diary

LAST STOP BEFORE POEM

Sometimes I see this it-looks-like-a-stopsign
Thing—or an erased stopsign—then the scene
Cuts to me and I'm running or else I'm all done
Running, finished, out of breath—or out of sigh—

And then, in the end, it happens. Again. Night
To night daily through the day I fade: by
Mocking myself I make myself enjoy—
Quickie spasms of dream. Then squirm, in my seat,

When the vids spritz bits from some terminal stage
—PBS: "AIDS Victims' Deliriums." They dance
Their booty. They shake that thing. Turn! turn! Retreat:

Death is such an easy cure for the plagued
Future. And time alone survives that present tense
These endstopped enjambments must wait to create.

(CASTRATION ENVY #21)
DOES THE SWORDSWALLOWER
SHIT PLOWSHARES?

Sure: the more me, the more morituri.
Mine duels his hand; some scroll of manliness,
Whose downfall almost dolored us. Though
Soon, up the brain tanks, gracias oozed.

The hair is a cohort of this. The hair,
Or the beard, a creditcard used as a napkin,
Swiping off a chin. "My adam's apple's agog!"
Quote: Exclude before you begin the male

Because it is vile. "The heart in common
Is the heart withheld," another recommends;
Hey here comes my favorite human-razed future.

Xerox of course a tapeworm lost inside
A hunchback, I squirm manfully on.
Deep in the direction known as thumbsdown.

EUCLID ALONE

Androids strolling up Everest will know
How harder it was for us to care, to cuddle
Visits from that summit within. The pique
Of pickups is endless. And when our oxygen

Thins to a pin who cares who's x who's y—
That altered acme stares at me—icily—
That game where time (come to theme) recombines
To dial them new stars night never fell on: it

Beads up as my eye, friend planet. Who like
The sate—crazed by my birth's first trip at bat—
A pork genus cordless vibrator whose tip

Whose tongue exbunged from your hinder heart, wet
With non-umbrageous plus-signs or what?
(But can we touch each other's thwart I thought.)

NIGHT AND THE NAKED
(for Rochelle)

The filmfestival swept beyond us as we kissed
Oh roundrobin panel where we went goodbye
Since then the weight (savored) of noncoincidence
As if each lightningbolt were secretly aimed at

A matchstick but were we ever on target as that
Whenever we meet now in the bar part or the
Restaurant part or the video part or the disco
Part or the atrium of this night I fear our parts our

Roles I mean because what if we you and me
Were cast to closeup the scene the street the strobe
Stabs of rain frying our profiles for future ref

Literals straight off a wanted poster of Janus
Because or would we just stand there thunderfucked
Trying to remember our name ends in applause

I'm blond which means my hair gives a shower to my face
Or is it wasserfall or 2 leash-burgers to go oh
Muy footbutch and anyway I am the guy right who
En-route to AKA a fungus minuet meets an andy

Which flicks back its eyelash crucifix and says
I come to touch you all ways but en passant
Like boohoo bruisers cruising Lost and Found Depts
But what about Marlene about the twins who want

To gaze at each other through a keyhole or Keith
What about them the andy says get out of it that's
No pocket for the slit-rilkes and shard-kafkas

That's watching the sockhop heave the voxpop vomit
May they meet sweeter than soon in that room
I say and point back where the streets are full of cities

HELP

The vestigial boomerang fur taps at the window of blank
    pennies.
It does this to help me use up the last words in my note-
    book.

MY EPITAPH

WANT TO EARN
BIG MONEY CARVING
TOMBSTONES? CALL NOW
FOR DETAILS:
317 1040*

*unfortunately snow or grass covers
    most of the number.

POEM!

Shh, you'll wake up the stains on my bedsheets.

PSYCHOPATHOLOGY OF
THE POWERTOOL WEEKEND
(NEOCOLONIALISM #5)

So—as the depth of the adieu—on my forehead
Shows, or my—signature, lopped off at—the wrist
Witnesses: ah, more quantum formulae scrawled
—You doodled margins of my christian bible! For

Like that drop of venom that longs to hang from
The comma although, cream of that snootiness
Magazine-covers sic us toward, my reflection
My joy is just (gloss to amuse) this world which,

Built on zoos, can't last. Or at least not till
The herd steered by its wounds disinherit
All I seize surmise of deepest tiptoe! Poo:

I lack the face you evolved to paw, Joe Blow,
The figure those fingers of yours grew for, Meg Smith.
I got no legit to forget it either, no greater esthetic.

MOTHER TERESA TREATS
TERRORISTS TO TAFFY

The A rack and the O thumbscrew, the
E pincers. Yeah, I brandingiron, U electrodes.
World I am defeatist of—elysium—
You eviscerate asterisks like me:

Pick up that hotline in your hushed-up highrise,
Higher-ups! I videopoemed them please
But did God's Little Guru LISTEN? Nope
So, tipping my head sideways as if trying

To pour it into the ear's cup I hung up. Oh
To fix my thought on 2 fingers giving
The peace sign inside my mouth nose ass—

Or whatever other orifice they fit—'s
Fine with me. Neutron bomb has the same
Theory. Our entrails is taller than we.

DE PRESIDENT OF DESCENT
(NEOCOLONIALISM #16)

'Insomnia, so I shot a few natives.'
Still, dawn has its palliatives; the cast sky
Lobs bullseye haloes; bursts of overview below
That pit whose voice timbers my spine: but why

Dis-niche this idol/this fiction called me? Which
A fluke, a fault, a streak of makeup down
A mirror where a stroke victim leaned to kiss—
Oh say the not right-out-of-it, say know.

Tongue: lightswitch of the body. Head: ha.
I'm serious! Every fable's a linear
Of topplings. And what falls first? Neck second

—I guess. Torso—torso off of groin—goes
And so on downwards—downwards—thighs knees et al.
The feet are a final ruins; the toes, shards.

PART THREE

Go from me: I am one of those, who fall.

—Johnson

MALE MENOPAUSE POEM

How as to lean my non-eon on autumn's roan
Undoing, to smile while the stymies crawl
All over me and the prismatic blindfold
Around my testicles squeaks: guess this house

No longer knows which door I am. The window
We were, does it remember its view? You-or-I
Saw so little out there; what future only
Catnap glimpses, of whose further nightmare . . .

Doorknobs worn to doornubs—grey stubble on
Gaunt armpits—lists like that litter this earth.
A lattice of graves greets me or is kind to me;

My hair plowed with parents, their protracted
Smoothings of some poor, tuckablanket bed.
As said each road I find in your face is fled.

Tying the pimp in dreams to a lamppost
His tuxedo wet with wheedled kisses, can
I wake up sucking the footprints of toilets
In jails that glitter like crash-dived marquees.

A dog appears in call letters on my skin.
Twin worlds, who exchange threats via scoreboard
I rival this night, this fight to the death
With enough leftover, ooze for twosies yet.

Either even, I wish I could put on take off
My clothes without first saying to my cock
"Excuse me, is this yours," while the stars

The collected no-shows of eternity, rise.
Hey, remember the way painters gauge perspective?
Me, I cut the thumb off and throw it at stuff.

SCHOOL FOR INSOMNIA

A bed of nails a manicurist hurls polish at—
The colors, liquid, thinking of a high tide I wonder
If it can remember the Primal Scene it relives
Again and again in pangs of ebb that plethora

Moment of what trance—conception—or are we
Out of source now, free, all pasts forgot as easily
As adults will plow a path through a children's
Birthday party—their pink lit-once, lit-twice,

Lit-five-times cake not stopping this progress, not
Even for a step that guesses what our heels could
Make of these tiny candles, crunch as crayons—

The colors, of evening then night are flames I fall
Tranq-sank in, the miniaturization of dust continues,
Night lies down on a bed of nails or stars—

A VIRGINSAINT AND A
SAINTVIRGIN SHARE A HALO
A WHILE: A MEMORY
(for Elaine Equi)

It was the onset of a golden headset
Our thought from covetous egypts took flight (suite)
Not so the veins' isle-lopped dictation
The sea that amanuensis with illegible gloves

But who wrote my pose throes over the white dot of
A desert's collectiste saliva whereon
A blindness bandaged by bats became dawn or
Was that oase-false face my scrotalskull gaze

The fever of eyecharts is distant tonight
This is my haiku scar this is my soft
Repeated sincere desire for fart-fairy confabs

Ah no abhorred form of present tense you see
That halo our askew nuked free is dead
Is circumscribed solely by the absence of head

A jet falls on a cow.
Part of the animal sticks out and twitches like the
    usual closeups of the hero's jaw.
Children I admire play in the crushed cow's shadow.
And even the plane itself has been left atop the skel-
    etonized milk-giver,
clouding one's dreams of a bloodless coup.

Stabbed by an elephant lens
On a meatless mattress I lie,
(Use a scalpel to trace my future;
The past, a suture) and die.

Spat at as often as the oil
Portrait of a moviestar on
The wall of a Death Row cell I fell
Into an abyss of worn-off

Sculptors' thumbs. Accidentally
Daily I cutted my throat on the
Drinking fountain. How was I

To know there is no justice,
Just a your-honor of trash?
I smile, a total inutile.

FOR IMELDA MARCOS

Whose hair mouth hands I long to be under
Like a painting a painter paints and repaints
Till and at last the canvas cracks apart then crash
Incredible shreddage, pale for all

Its color, its whole only in tatter: I want
To be gone on at like that by her. But
Won't the brush the play of such force across
Me obliterate those whatever forms I might

With the rough sketch of the heart have
Brought to connoisseurs critics crowds
Eager to offer prize: even if I were torn

Wantonly tossed in the dirt the street
Stepped on and lost, as lost as she is to me, I
Would rather under her feet be than their eyes.

LAST MOMENTS IN THE MASTERPIECE

Once aboard the world a venereal disease
The Beatles* gave you takes on new forms
And shows them how to elevate birth. But then
A pasture attends. The clothes fit the cows,

Though styles are better back in the barn, where
Some denouement mode monde meet as photos for
The magazine this poem has published or
Will I be the sum of misprints here.

That should suffice could hours need to suffer:
Our clock ye-gods toward arrival, medieval
Catapults release aim-things, whose same music

Is defter in sepia, that mooing hue, lit by fakes.
*Or Picasso, Gertrude Stein, Peter Schuyff, Der Fuhrer,
Or any other 3-syllable entity you'd prefer-er.

MORE BEST JOKES OF THE
DELPHIC ORACLE
"Eigentlich spricht die Sprache"
                    —Heidegger

I vow to live always at trash point: to
Waste my past talking about the weather
In mirrors, how they cloud or is it clear
With no certain referent to that what was

Forecast. Like Snow White's dust-draped stepmother
I smile up at the dictionary whispering
My favorite definition, down at the stove my
Worst recipe. The endproduct in me

Agrees. It and I are one in this blither
And, I believe, we echo something endless,
Eine global vocal. Will those lips ever

Repent this recorded message. Lips
That remain a mere testimonial
To the inchworm's socialization progress.

HITLER SKELETON GOLDPLATED
(FROM *TREASURES OF THE C.I.A. MUSEUM*,
EDITED BY HILTON KRAMER, WITH AN
INTRODUCTION BY JERZY KOSINSKI.
RANDOM HOUSE/IBM, 1984)

What falls from the drunken pliers of my nose
President-pit pope-rind police-bone
Is all they got on this fucking menu
Always the pure provend of more more more

The piss tease of masterpiece ass
The missionary position is there to catch you
If you drip off that mosquito plaque I guess
Gumming some gifthorse's defectual innocence

The gunfire in the hills is old and I
Am one pile of shit which will never excrete a human
Hey Parliament Congress Politburo

My cock/my KGB has it on lasertape
The moon posing between the horns of a bull
Two hymens touching through milk

In the collided night, sate with pool. The
Truly gooey goes if an armpit could point
This is what it would point at. Same veneer
Where I chew your girdle and gum your bra

—Crates to pack Proteus in, the days
Oops. The fall took all the minutehand. So
The with you will die and the without me live,
Like a letter mailed inside a folded

Up postagestamp. What do you hear from whom?
Softer than the pins stuck into cacti by
Rubbing my sores on the Lot's Wifes displayed

Or shit. Mud. Crud. It's milkingtime:
Sometimes those udder-things have to be cleaned off.
So you use the first squirts to do it with.

The butterfingers things that hold us know
To plunk the gut strings of your suturous
Lobotomy lyre—but if it is to pore
Iota'd digits through a wall with no elses

In it I do not. Who scans test tubes for
The fatal ripple of my beauty finds
That long meant mirror has fled in error since
In their clone alphabet seems I'm z:

This crystalball bilge/ouch mosaic of
Out of touch omens will not tune true too as
My leavetaking leaking everywhere sees

A 'puter oh! inventory zeroes.
Why try to guess which one comes last? Just zoom
Your monitor. The past the gist of it gets us.

NONREQUITALS
(to ----)

Each night you transfer
my fingernails to my toes,
my toenails to my fingers.

And if the magician
waving simple cardtricks
disembowel himself somehow,
through some slight slip in skill—

Evening's when we live, mostly.
Before an unhatched iceberg
I preen my scars.

You bade his only face brought in
on a slice of camera
—but affixed blue earrings
to a whiter skull . . .

No-one will return
my toenails to my toes,
my fingernails to my fingers.
No-one will rip up the list
of those loved by those not on the list.

THE HEROES CROWD EACH OTHER
AT THE GATE

But this cryptic impulse to eclipse a map
While voiceovers avail one's profile or
The blindfolds floating to the ground smile
The vegetation shiver a little

Light has not accustomed swimmingpools to this
Glitter and illiterates with gold records know
And all our next door to door neighbors the Nukes
Family who play charades to remember

Each other's names they feel it hie vie die
Across that oversuffice of knife their life
Santa's reindeer sneer down from the sky as

Guiding your foot with my hand to its mark
My face I reflect on how this world which
Does not consist of more you's than you does

THE FROOTLOOPS OF CONSOLATION

One of those landscapes that explicate Eliot.
Up: evening-pubescent clouds tuft-about a sun
That rusts like a shelf of spare parts for god
Or such, who flee with perhapses as pitstops:

The airport that sold me all I know is gone now.
The welcome-mats that were so cheap (a foreign
Manufacturer had misspelled them)—that whole symbol
Semblage/emblem forum: bereft of forms I bend

Across this blindfold's bliss land and see
My soul or a lobotomy spaghetti
—Choice of terms—crawl by. By what small light the

Day has not betrayed you step so long among
The Magritte-lit map. A single tight-rope
Stretches between its houses, threading the keyholes.

AT THE NIXON MEMORIAL
(Nixon Beach, California, USA)
(Just minutes away from OzymandiasLand®)

They say that robots simply have to slap mirrors
Up against their voice grilles to try and make sure they're
Not breathing, whereas I kiss caress this monument,
This eternal mall on which Herod has chalked x,

This statue stands for more than blowjobs in spaceships
Or all our names have razed, aimless oceans frying,
While a scab forms on the world's microphone: praise him.
Oh orgasm you robot's vomit I come unheck.

(tape gap) lie back gunked motel whispers dream . . . back (gasp)
To be the genre of my frontier. One hears aborigines
Prefer to, er, fornicate. Money for thought, nyet?

Will the army vote to internalize its camouflage;
At the Reagan Rotunda Paul Valéry allowed how
Shorelines change too, rumorous as their dunes.

> *Le changement des rives en rumeur.*
> —Le Cimetière marin

THE SCULPTURE
(for Star Black)

We stood there nude embracing while the sculptor
Poked and packed some sort of glop between us
Molding fast all the voids the gaps that lay
Where we'd tried most to hold each other close

Under the merge of your breasts and my chest
There remained a space above the place our
Bellies met but soon that clay or plaster
Of paris or state of the art polymer

Filled every hollow which we long to fit
Then we were told to kiss hug hug harder
And then our heat would help to harden it

We stood there fused more ways than lovers know
Before the sculptor tore us away
Forced us to look at what had made us so whole

Pinky Brown must marry Rose Wilson
to keep her mouth shut about the murder
which the cops don't know wasn't no accident—

Pinky has a straight razor for slashing,
a vial of acid for throwing into,
a snitch's face. He dies in the end. The end

of the book, I mean—where, on the last page,
Rose snuffles on home from church to pray
that her Pinky has left her pregnant . . .

Now, this kid—if he was ever born—joined
a skiffle group in '62 called Brighton
Rockers, didn't make it big, though,

just local dances and do's. Rose,
pink, brown, all nonelemental colors, shades
of shame, melancholy, colors which, you

get caught loving too much, you get sent up
to do time—time, that crime you didn't,
couldn't commit! even if you weren't

born, even and if your dad he died with
the sneer, unsmooched his punk's pure soul, unsaved . . .
Every Sunday now in church Rose slices

her ring-finger off, onto the collection-plate;
once the sextons have gathered enough
bodily parts from the congregation, enough

to add up to an entire being, the priest sub-
stitutes that entire being for the one
on the cross: they bring Him down in the name

of brown and rose and pink, sadness
and shame, His body, remade, is yelled at
and made to get a haircut, go to school,

study, to do each day like the rest
of us crawling through this igloo of hell,
and laugh it up, show pain a good time,

and read Brighton Rock by Graham Greene.

REFUSING AN INVITATION
TO THE MASKED BALL

No knees forcep my tongue to you. Met when
It dims like hesitant fever over
That oasis-in-a-swimsuit, what studious mirage
Rises. Mist is the dog augments the scene.

Whose collapsar sponsors these closeups?—
The escapes in forced moonlight of the prince
At his powerboat throughout alpine lakes chased
Or so the whisper ran, rotting in attendance:

May I hang the fur coat on the beehive? thanks—
That place that fills the map that swamps the front
Seats of the Royal Starship rendezvous

Holds perhaps. Till then, scintilla antenna
Omniscient thistle of my Etcetera Dracula,
A smile across that which we would share, flesh.

Some poems in this book may look like personae/dramatic monologs, but I don't intend them as such. Please take this into account when you read them.

PART ONE

"[T]he *fin de siècle* of the nineteenth century . . . seemed as worn-out to the avant-garde modernists of 1912 as it seems topical again to the present current of postmodernism."—Hans Robert Jauss (*Yale French Studies* 74)

page:

1 Il Vittoriale: D'Annunzio's retirement villa. *Sempre Sera.*

3 John Gray: author of *Silverpoints* (1893). Ada Leverson in her preface to *Letters to the Sphinx from Oscar Wilde* (1930) writes that Gray was "then considered the incomparable poet of the age." Line 7: he was thought by some to be the model for Wilde's hero. (The choice: Dorian or Jesus—as Barbey d'Aurevilly posed it to Huysmans, "the muzzle of a pistol or the foot of the Cross": Gray was ordained a Catholic priest in 1901.)

4 Title: of a work by Rops.

5 Flecker: Parnassianism (his list: "Hérédia, Leconte de Lisle, Samain, Henri de Régnier, and Jean Moréas"); le vice anglais (the home version); death at age 30 (consumption).

6 Inspired by Hagiwara's *A Barren Area.* My attempt at *hon'yaku-chō*, a favorite mode of the poet, according to Hiroaki Sato, who defines it as "translation style . . . writings that read like clumsy translations." Line 1: "J'ai tendu des cordes de clocher à clocher . . ."—Rimbaud.

7 Title: a phrase of Mallarmé's explication of *Ses purs ongles très haut dédiant leur onyx. . . .*

9 Title (excluding the parenthesis): of a work by Khnopff. Line 14: 'What's named between the knees': I can't recall where this quote comes from, or if in fact it is a quote.

10 Title: of a work by John Martin.

12 The Marchesa Casati "was painted by fifty or more artists, from Boldini to Van Dongen" (Philippe Jullian). It would make a fascinating exhibit to see all of these portraits hung, one after another, upon a nail protruding from my forehead.

14 Failed translation of Mallarmé's *Brise Marine*.

15 Parenthetical part of title: "Votre âme est un paysage choisi . . ." —the first line of Verlaine's *Clair de Lune*.

16 Line 8: "Exclus-en si tu commences / Le réel parce que vil" —Mallarmé.

PART TWO

"The important thing is what one makes of one's nihilism."—Gottfried Benn

20 Lines 1–3: "He wrote about the demonic city, the wretchedness of suburbs, bodies fished out of rivers, and distress in the hospitals."— Armin Arnold, writing about George Heym. Lines 9–10: Getty Museum richest in USA. Anyway, most 'masterpieces' in museums are forgeries; the real stuff is sequestered by billionaires.

30 Title: "Euclid alone has looked on Beauty bare."—Millay.

34 Neocolonialism: Outremer was Europe's first attempt to create a "USA": it fell apart after 2 or 3 centuries, overrun by 'the natives' . . . xerox for us? Ah the comminution of this latter Crusade; me, crumb.

PART THREE

"My canvases are painted in a dark room and cannot stand the light of day."—Strindberg

44 Title: of a painting by Alberto Savinio.

45 Title: originally "For Claudia"—the 'real' person who inspired it . . .

but the poem itself is so unreal, so un-anything, that I think an un-title—an anti-title—is better . . . but maybe I'm wrong . . . maybe it's a case of that old saying (I quote Peter Stitt's revised version): "penny wise, mussolini foolish". . . .

47 Epigraph: "Speech is language made literal" or "Talk talks till it's true" or "Tongue is the only word the tongue says for real" or something like that. ("Language is Delphi."—Novalis.)

48 Parenthetical part of title: does this book exist? or did I only imagine reading it? What do you think?

49 This form was adumbrated by Octavio Paz in *Renga* (1971).

52 Title: a phrase by Abel Gance; as quoted in the screenplay for *Hitler: A Film from Germany*.

54 Line 14: what better way to end a poem about RN than with an act of theft? A seaside mausoleum, so the Valéry seemed appropriate. With thoughts of the Shelley sonnet's last line.

THE IOWA POETRY PRIZE WINNERS

1987

Elton Glaser, *Tropical Depressions*

Michael Pettit, *Cardinal Points*

1988

Mary Ruefle, *The Adamant*

Bill Knott, *Outremer*